Discover and Share

Pets

D0452701

Angela Royston

W
FRANKLIN WATTS
LONDON•SYDNEY

About this book

The **Discover and Share** series enables young readers to read about familiar topics independently. The books are designed to build on children's existing knowledge while providing new information and vocabulary. By sharing this book, either with an adult or another child, young children can learn how to access information, build word recognition skills and develop reading confidence in an enjoyable way.

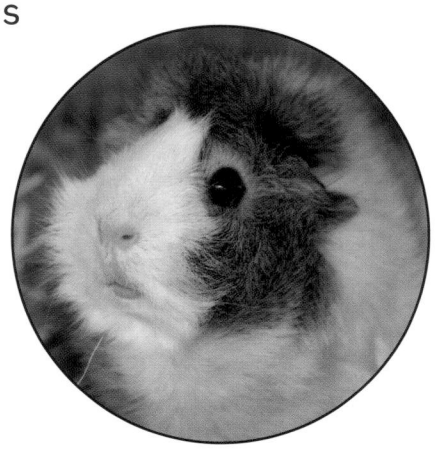

Reading tips

- Begin by finding out what children already know about the topic. Encourage them to talk about it and take the opportunity to introduce vocabulary specific to the topic.
- Each image is explained through two levels of text. Confident readers will be able to read the higher level text independently, while emerging readers can try reading the simpler sentences.
- Check for understanding of any unfamiliar words and concepts. Inexperienced readers might need you to read some or all of the text to them. Encourage children to retell the information in their own words.
- After you have explored the book together, try the quiz on page 22 to see what children can remember and to encourage further discussion.

Contents

What is a pet? 4
Looking after a pet 6
Friendly dogs 8
Cool cats 10
Rabbits in the garden 12
Hamster home 14
Hungry lizards 16
Fish tank 18
Visiting the vet 20
Quiz 22
Glossary 23
Index 24

MORAY COUNCIL
LIBRARIES &
INFO.SERVICES
20 38 43 39
Askews & Holts
J636.0887

Words in **bold** are in the glossary on page 23.

What is a pet?

A pet is a tame animal that usually lives in your home. Tame animals are not afraid of people.

There are lots of different kinds of pet. Hamsters are small. This dog is a Great Dane. It is very big!

Pets live with us. Some pets are small, but some are big.

Looking after a pet

Wild animals look after themselves, but pets need people to look after them.

Pets need clean water to drink and food to eat. They need space to exercise and clean **bedding** to sleep in.

You need to take care of a pet. Pets need clean water to drink.

Friendly dogs

Dogs like to go for walks. They wag their tail when they are happy.

Dogs like to go for a long walk every day. If you throw a ball, the dog will run after it.

You can tell how a dog feels. When it is happy it holds its tail up high and wags it from side to side.

Cool cats

Cats like to spend time on their own, but they also like to be stroked. They may **purr** when they are stroked.

Cats chase anything that moves quickly, such as a toy mouse or a ball.

Some cats purr when they are stroked.

Rabbits in the garden

This rabbit lives in the garden. It likes to eat the grass.

Many pet rabbits live outside in the garden.
They have a special **hutch** to shelter in.

Rabbits nibble the grass and keep it short.

Hamster home

A hamster likes a cage with lots of space to play. The cage keeps the hamster safe.

The hamster has everything it needs in the cage. It sucks water from a special water bottle.

A hamster is safe in its cage.
It has all the things
it needs here.

Hungry lizards

Some people keep lizards as pets.
A lizard is a type of **reptile**.
A reptile's skin is covered with
hard **scales**.

A lizard eats insects, such as **crickets.**
It also likes pieces of vegetable and fruit.

A lizard has scaly skin. It eats insects and fruit.

Fish tank

Lots of different pet fish live together in a tank.

Fish eat special fish **pellets**. When pellets are dropped into the water, the fish come to the surface to eat them.

Lots of fish live in this tank.
The fish swim up to get the food.

Visiting the vet

Sometimes a pet becomes ill. Then you have to put your pet in a special **carrier** and take it to a vet.

The vet may give your pet medicine to make it better.

Pets sometimes get ill. You should take them to a vet.

Quiz

1. What is this cat doing?

2. How does a dog show it is happy?

3. What does this rabbit like to eat?

4. How many fish can you see in this picture?

Glossary

bedding dried grass or other material which animals sleep on
carrier a cage or basket for carrying something
cricket a jumping insect
hutch a cage designed for rabbits
pellets small pieces of a mixture of many types of food
purr gentle growling sound made by a cat
reptile a large group of animals which have a dry, scaly skin. Snakes and lizards are reptiles.
scales small pieces of hard skin
wild not owned or looked after by people

Answers to quiz:
1. It is drinking water.
2. It wags its tail.
3. Grass.
4. Three.

Index

ball 9, 10

cage 14, 15
cats 10–11

dogs 8–9

fish 18–19

hamsters 4, 14–15
hutch 13

insects 17

lizards 16–17

purr 10, 11

rabbits 12–13

tail 8, 9
tame animals 4
tank 18, 19

vet 20–21

wild animals 6

This edition copyright ©
Franklin Watts 2014

Franklin Watts
338 Euston Road
London
NW1 3BH

Franklin Watts Australia
Level 17/207 Kent Street
Sydney
NSW 2000

ISBN 978 1 4451 3647 9
Library ebook ISBN 978 1 4451 2499 5

Dewey number: 636'.0887

A CIP catalogue record for this book is available from the British Library.

Series Editor: Julia Bird
Series Advisor: Karina Law
Series Design: Basement68

Picture credits: Ermolaev Alexander /Shutterstock: 11. Arco/Nature PL: 13. Yuri Arcurs/Dreamstime: 4, 17, 23. Art Directors and Trip/Alamy: 15. Breti Critchley/Dreamstime: 18. Eldacarin/Dreamstime: 3b, 9. Imageman/Shutterstock: 12, 22bl. Tatiana Katsai/Shutterstock: front cover. Lusoimages/Shutterstock: 20. Julia Mashkova/istockphoto: 7, 22tl. Mkoudis/Dreamstime: 2, 6. Guy Moberly/Alamy: 8, 22tr. Papilio/Alamy: 3c, 14. Artem and Olga Sapegin/Shutterstock: 5. Benjamin Simeneta/Dreamstime: 1, 10. Brocke Whatnall/Shutterstock: 3t, 16. Glenn Young/Shutterstock: 19, 22br.

Every attempt has been made to clear copyright. Should there be any inadvertent omission please apply to the publisher for rectification. All rights reserved. No part of this publication may be reproduced, stored in a retrieval system, or transmitted in any form or by any means, electronic,mechanical, photocopy, recording or otherwise, without the prior written permission of the copyright owner.

Printed in China

Franklin Watts is a division of
Hachette Children's Books,
an Hachette UK company.
www.hachette.co.uk